LONDON *to* PARIS
IN TEN MINUTES

the eurostar story

IMAGES
PUBLISHING

JEANNE GRIFFITHS

JEANNE GRIFFITHS has been senior editor in several publishing companies, including *Time-Life*, London, and has worked on over 100 titles, including the three-volume *Annotated Shakespeare,* which she produced for American and UK publishers. She is the author of *The Photographer's Project Book*, *The Official Guide to Epping Forest* and, with Judy Allen, *The Book of the Dragon;* and has compiled seven anthologies. She has also contributed chapters to other books, including *Conran's House Book*, and writes regularly for many national magazines and newspapers. For five years she was the editor of *Country* magazine and *Your Money* magazine, and presently compiles three magazines for customers of major British companies.

Jeanne has a passion for train journeys, and has made many around Europe.

First published in Great Britain 1995 by

Images Publishing (Malvern) Ltd

Upton upon Severn

Worcestershire

British Library Cataloguing in Publication Data

A catalogue record for this book is available
from the British Library

ISBN 1 897817 47 9

Designed and Produced by Images Publishing (Malvern) Ltd
Printed and Bound in Great Britain by Lawrence-Allen Colour Printers Ltd

C O N T E N T S

ACKNOWLEDGEMENTS

I am indebted to many people for their help with this book, in particular to Catherine Whiting of Images Publishing Ltd, who did so much of the initial research and ground work and who edited the text, and to Tony Harold, also of Images, for his encouragement, enthusiasm and support. I am grateful to Peter Akehurst of Wizard Productions, who made the film on *Eurostar* and who allowed me access to his research and pictures.

My thanks also to the staff of GEC Alsthom, Belfort, France; to the European Passenger Services engineers, in particular to Gerry Arnold; to Jim Rowe and Malcolm Parsons of EPS media relations department who supplied much of the information, answered my many questions, who kindly read the text prior to publication, and who arranged for me to experience the train journey to Paris; and to Nasima Hussain of EPS who kindly supplied many of the pictures from EPS's picture library.

The chapter on the Channel Tunnel would not have been possible without one valuable and authoritative source, *The Tunnel: The Story of the Channel Tunnel 1802-1994* by the late Donald Hunt.

I would also like to thank Jill Campion for reading the manuscript through; Andrew Best and Jackie Hunt for their assistance; and, last but not least, my husband Dermot Hayes and son Joshua who were so supportive and thoroughly neglected while I wrote it.

Courtesy of Peter Akehurst.

A new age of international travel began on 14th November 1994. *Eurostar* services officially opened to provide the first ever high speed city centre to city centre rail link between Britain and mainland Europe. It was an historic moment: London to Paris in just three hours non-stop, and London to Brussels in three hours fifteen minutes. Offering frequency, reliability, comfort and the opportunity to capitalise on travelling time, this new service immediately caught the public imagination, attracting thousands of business travellers and holiday-makers. And that was just the beginning. International trains will soon be leaving from cities all over the British Isles, day and night, to speed passengers straight through to mainland Europe.

Of course, all this would not have been possible without the existence of the Channel Tunnel, an extraordinary feat of engineering. First conceived in the 1800s, political differences and financial wranglings meant that it took nearly two hundred years to bring the project to fruition. Construction eventually began on 15th December 1987; and, just under three years later, the two countries were linked for the first time since the Ice Age. The Tunnel was inaugurated by Her Majesty Queen Elizabeth II and France's President François Mitterrand on 6th May 1994. At a cost of around £9 billion, the Tunnel must be acknowledged as a remarkable achievement – and a political miracle.

The Tunnel is, however, only a means to an end. It is the concept of making the journey straight through from one great city centre to another, at speeds suited to today's pace, that is exciting. Such a journey should also be made in style, in a form which takes travel within Europe into the 21st century. And what is better suited for the purpose than these masterpieces of futuristic engineering – the fastest, longest and most luxurious forms of earthbound travel in the world – the *Eurostar* trains?

Courtesy of EPS

CHAPTER ONE

HISTORY IN THE MAKING

In January 1993, the first of a new generation of trains left the production line for testing. With its aerodynamic nose, brightly painted in canary yellow, *Eurostar PS1* was on the tracks. Here was a train capable of running on the different rail networks of three countries, at speeds of up to 300 kilometres per hour, while needing only one driver.

Eurostar is the latest in a long and often arduous development of trains. The origin of railways dates back at least to Roman times, when ruts were dug into roads to keep wheeled vehicles on track. By the 15th century, miners in Europe were using timber tracks to provide a smooth route for their barrows. 1787 saw the invention of the L-section iron plate rail, which transformed underground transport for mines in Britain and led to the development of using iron wheels on iron rails: the consequent loss of friction, and therefore resistance between wheel and rail, meant that wagons could take heavier loads pulled by one horse.

The harnessing of steam power brought about the next major stage of development. Steam creates a vacuum against which atmospheric pressure reacts to move a piston, and was found to be an effective method of pumping out water from mines. Thomas Newcomen was one of the first to develop an engine for this purpose in 1712; but it was Richard Trevithick, a Cornishman, who designed a steam engine in which the pressure of the steam was directly responsible for moving the piston, while allowing the exhaust to discharge into the atmosphere rather than condense. Steam at this high pressure created much more power from a smaller cylinder – the concept of a steam locomotive engine was in sight. Trevithick's first successful road locomotive appeared in 1801; two years later he was involved in the design and building of what is now accepted as the first steam locomotive to be tried on rails – at the Coalbrookdale ironworks.

The first successful locomotive to run on rails, 1803.
Courtesy of The Science Museum/Science & Society Picture Library.

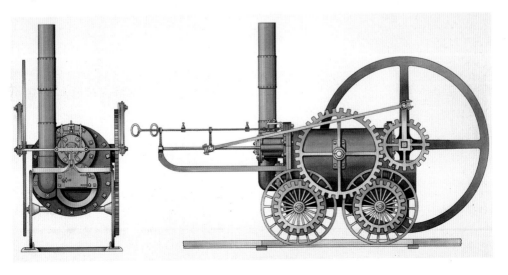

Richard Trevithick's last engine, Catch as Catch Can, built in 1808, ran on rails for a short time the following year, hauling passenger-carrying wagons for entertainment in Euston Square, London.
Courtesy of The Science Museum/Science & Society Picture Library.

But it is George Stephenson, born in 1781, in Newcastle-upon-Tyne, who is most commonly heralded as the 'inventor' of steam trains. As enginewright for a group of collieries, it was he who finally addressed the problem of inefficiency due to condensation and simplified the transmission of thrust to the driving wheels. He also added a basic system of springing, which partly cushioned the locomotive, improving adhesion and reducing the number of rail breaks. His railway system for the Hetton Colliery, County Durham, which opened in 1822, incorporated horses and stationary steam engines to help haul wagons up gradients.

Stephenson then met Edward Pease, one of the promoters of the Stockton & Darlington Railway. Designed for moving coal, the railway's

A print from the original painting by John Dobbins showing the opening of the Stockton & Darlington Railway, 1825.
Courtesy of NRM/Science & Picture Library.

feasibility caused so much debate that an Act of Parliament had to be sought for its development. Stephenson's engine, *Locomotion*, was used to haul the inaugural train to Stockton on 27th September 1825. It pulled 600 guest passengers in 38 wagons a distance of 21 miles and reached a speed of 15 miles per hour. Within 18 months, the success of the new railway had been responsible for halving the price of coal in Stockton and the railway company was already making a profit.

However, in the first eight years of real railways, all passenger travel was still horse drawn, with stagecoach owners paying tolls to use the railway's track. The Stockton & Darlington Act had allowed owners of land adjoining the line to build their own branch lines. This soon proved dangerously impractical, as use of the lines needed to be properly co-ordinated by one company. And so the Stockton & Darlington effectively became the first of a new style of railway company, to be followed by many others.

Stephenson had already been approached by the directors of the proposed Liverpool & Manchester railway, the first to carry both freight and passengers and to join two major cities. To find the best locomotive for the route, the directors organised a competition. Each locomotive had to travel 37.5 miles twice – representing the return trip between Manchester and Liverpool. Stephenson entered his new *Rocket* engine, the first locomotive to incorporate the principal features necessary to propel a machine by steam successfully and economically. Needless to say, the engine won the competition and took part in the opening ceremony on 15th September 1830. Within three months of its opening, more than half the stagecoaches that ran between Liverpool and Manchester were off the road. Earlier in the same year, a short passenger service had been inaugurated by the Canterbury & Whitstable Railway. The age of passenger-carrying trains had arrived.

George Stephenson's Rocket, *the first engine designed to haul passengers and freight.*
Courtesy of The Science Museum/Science & Society Picture Library.

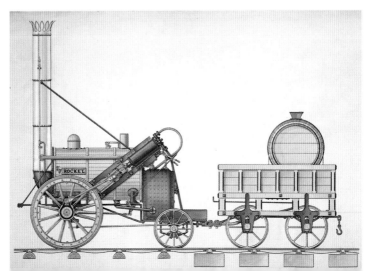

The Great Western Railway, engineered by Isambard Kingdom Brunel, joined Britain's capital with Bristol, considered in the 1830s as the second most important city. Brunel used a unique broad gauge of 7 feet ¼ inch, although it was later converted to the standard gauge of 4 feet 8½ inch.
Courtesy of NRM/Science & Society Picture Library.

Once they had proved a commercial success, other passenger railways sprang up and greater distances were covered. The London to Birmingham line – to which Stephenson's son Robert was appointed Chief Engineer – opened in 1837, and Isambard Kingdom Brunel's Great Western Railway opened the following year.

Between 1845 and 1847, Parliament sanctioned 8,592 miles of track – about one third of what was actually built during that time. Bridges were built, houses demolished to make way for track, towns grew up around the railways, and railways became big employers. Workers began to commute and suburbs sprang up. The railways played a major role in re-shaping life in Britain, socially, commercially and topographically. This development was not unique. By the 1870s, railways had become the principal means of transport in Europe, North America, India, Russia and Australia.

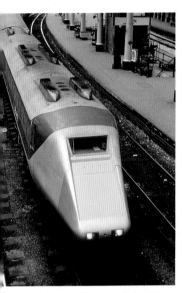

BR's ill-fated Advanced Passenger Train. Only three trainsets were ever built. Courtesy of NRM/Science & Society Picture Library.

Steam began to give way to diesel in the late 1920s, based on the first diesel locomotives developed by the German Rudolph Diesel. Other countries, such as France, experimented with electric trains. By 1955 the French railway company SNCF demonstrated that electric trains were capable of speeds of up to 200 miles per hour. The idea of electric power was not new: the first practical electric railway had been demonstrated in Berlin in 1879, and electric trains – cleaner, if more expensive to run – had been used on London's Underground since the late nineteenth century. But Britain was slower than its European counterparts to electrify its main network and diesel or diesel-electric still ruled the day.

While traditionalists' feared that conventional trains still had great potential, commercialists called for something new and faster. British Rail tested its first High Speed Train, then a diesel, in 1973, setting a world record for diesel trains of 143 miles per hour, which still stands. The following decade BR introduced the electric Advanced Passenger Train (APT). In theory, this train was capable of reaching 155 miles per hour and could maintain these speeds even round bends on existing track. In practice, it did not work and had to be

The Flying Scotsman, the name of an express train introduced in 1928, went on to claim the world record for length of regular daily non-stop work – London to Edinburgh. The train seen here in 1987, was the second of a new generation of diesel-electric High Speed Trains, making London to Edinburgh in 4½ hours. Courtesy of Quadrant Picture Library.

scrapped. The Japanese, meanwhile, laid a new line for their 12,000 hp high speed electric train to run between Tokyo and Osaka, a distance of 320 miles. Opened in 1964, the railway reduced the journey time to just three hours.

In 1981, from the technology developed in the 1950s, the French TGVs (*trains à grande vitesse*) came into service; these electric-powered trains ran on specially-built track and were capable of speeds of up to 160 miles per hour. Other European countries began to follow suit and so an infrastructure of high speed railways began to emerge.

Above: the first generation of French TGVs. The PSE (Paris Sud-Est), *with its orange livery, went into service in 1981; and is now used by an average of 55,000 people every day.*
Courtesy of Milepost 92½.

Below: the second generation – TGV Atlantique.
Courtesy of EPS.

CHAPTER TWO

EUROSTAR

On 11th September 1981, France and the United Kingdom announced the launch of studies into a fixed link across the Channel which would join the two countries together for the first time in over 10,000 years. Five years later, in January 1986, Margaret Thatcher and François Mitterrand announced that they had chosen the Eurotunnel project – a dual rail tunnel for passenger trains and shuttles carrying both passenger-vehicles and freight.

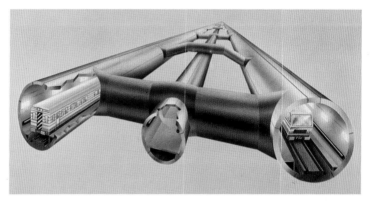

Artist's impression of the Eurotunnel project. Courtesy of EPS.

The Eurotunnel project gave railways a golden opportunity to develop their share of the cross-Channel travel market, while providing them with a prestigious route on which to operate Europe's first truly international high speed train. London to Paris (307 miles) in three hours, and London to Brussels (236 miles) in three hours fifteen minutes, was an exciting possibility. These times will become even faster when the new Belgium high speed link opens in 1997 and the British high speed link is built from the Tunnel to St Pancras, north London.

The idea of an international high speed link was put forward in October 1987, when the French Government announced its decision to build a high speed railway line from Paris to the Tunnel entrance via Lille. The British and Belgian authorities reacted quickly to the French news and the three countries joined forces to develop a new train that would take Europe, and train travel, into a new era.

January 1988 saw the formation of an International Project Group, which brought together the three railway networks – British Rail, France's SNCF and the Belgian SNCB – and the future manufacturers of what was then known as the Trans Manche Super Train (TMST). Based in Paris, the Group set out to define common standards, specifications and contracts; and, despite some initial apprehension, soon found that differing national characteristics proved highly complementary.

From the three consortia (Belgian, British and French), who originally worked together designing the Trans Manche Super Train, there emerged a single consortium led by the Anglo-French company, GEC Alsthom. The Group's influence increased with the acquisition of the British company Metro Cammell (Metcam) and Belgium's ACEC Transport. Other companies making up the consortium are: France's De Dietrich which built the body shells and assembled the motor trailers; Brush Electrical Machines Ltd of Loughborough for the asynchronous machines; and the Belgian BN Division of Bombardier Eurorail, for the construction of the two central trailers.

On 18th December 1989, the three railway networks signed a contract for an initial 31 trains. SNCF ordered 16 trains, each with 18 coaches, and SNCB ordered another four. European Passenger Services, then a wholly-owned subsidiary of British Rail, ordered 11 trains and a further seven 14-coach trains designed for the British network 'beyond London'; these trains, scheduled to be phased into service in early 1996, will initially extend the international service to Manchester, Birmingham, York, Newcastle and Edinburgh, stopping at major stations en route.

Each year over 60 million people journey between the UK and other countries in Europe. Traffic has tripled in the last 20 years. It is predicted that Eurostar trains will carry 15 million passengers a year by the turn of the century.

THE DESIGN

In 1988 the three networks launched an international competition to choose a group of Belgian, French and British designers to form a team under the French prize-winning industrial designer Roger Tallon, already renowned for his work on SNCF's *Corail* trains and the TGV *Atlantique*. Tallon was commissioned to design the livery of *Eurostar* and the carriages, while the Belgian Jacques Tilman worked on other parts of the train's interior. *Eurostar* differs from the TGV in that it is rounder and sleeker. The TGV, while it too has a distinctive nose, is a squarer train. The aerodynamic nose of *Eurostar* was designed by Briton Roger Jones, of

Eurostar *beside its predecessor, the TGV* Atlantique.
Courtesy of EPS.

Standard class coach. Courtesy of EPS.

First class coach. Courtesy of C. Whiting.

Jones Garrard, who also created the inside of the driver's cabin and the buffet and bar area.

For the interior, the designers chose a soft grey and bright yellow for the standard class coaches and pale blue for the washrooms. First class carriages have plush red and grey-striped carpet and a spacious seating arrangement – two seats on one side of the central aisles, and a single seat on the other. First class passengers can also use the specially-designed areas for business meetings, where four seats are set around a table equipped with a lamp.

Designed for maximum comfort, with footrests, reading lights and air-conditioning controls, *Eurostar* also has four telephone booths with cellular network phones which operate internationally, except while the train is in the Tunnel. They take credit cards and special *Eurostar* cards on sale in the buffet area.

Special places have been set aside for people in wheelchairs and all the train's and terminal facilities have been designed to conform with the needs of disabled passengers. On the train, there are baby changing facilities, two bar-buffets and a trolley service. Children's play areas can be created by fold-away seats. *Eurostar* even has its own tri-lingual monthly magazine.

The buffet area. Courtesy of C. Whiting.

Courtesy of EPS.

The *Eurostar* name and logo was designed by the international design agency Minale Tattersfield Design Strategy, which has offices in Paris and London. The three blue waves form an 'E', denoting the three European partners. The star, symbol of the future, balances the design and emphasises the excellence of the *Eurostar* service.

UNIFORMS

The uniforms were specially designed by the French *haute couture* house Pierre Balmain. Around 2,300 people in the three companies plus catering staff will wear the new uniforms, designed to pick up the distinctive yellow of *Eurostar's* exterior. Thirteen categories of staff are involved, from drivers to reception staff, and all of the uniforms will be wholly made within Europe.

Courtesy of EPS.

THE TECHNICALITIES

For the three railway networks and manufacturers, *Eurostar* was a great challenge – designing a high speed train that could run on three different national railway systems and in the Tunnel.

The Super Train that was to become *Eurostar* technically resembles its parent, the French TGV – an articulated train that can run at 186 miles (300 kilometres) per hour. One important difference, however, is that *Eurostar* is equipped with asynchronous electric motors, which are more robust, provide more power and deliver power at greater speeds. With a length of 1,294 feet (394 metres) *Eurostar* is also the longest high speed train, essentially to provide greater seating capacity.

While the track gauge – the width between the rails – is standard across most of Europe, the loading gauge – the amount of space needed by the train to allow it to clear bridges, tunnels and so on – differs. Because of this, *Eurostar* had to be compatible with the most restrictive gauge – the British gauge; this required changes to the airbag-suspension of the bogies – the wheels and axles which give pivoted support – as well as to the width of the coaches. Platform heights also vary (550 mm above the rails in France, 915 mm in Britain and 760 mm in Belgium); retractable foot-boards

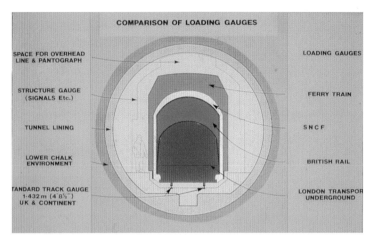

Courtesy of EPS.

at the doorways have therefore been designed to extend to different widths and heights so that passengers can board and alight from British and continental platforms, as well as reaching the walkways along the sides of the Channel Tunnel.

A side and overhead plan of the power car and four coaches of the Trans-Manche Super Train, now known as Eurostar. *Each trainset consists of a power car, 18 trailers, and a second power car at the end. The outer end of each trailer car (called R1 and R18) is also powered from equipment located at the end of the coach which is mounted on a motor bogie.*
Courtesy of EPS.

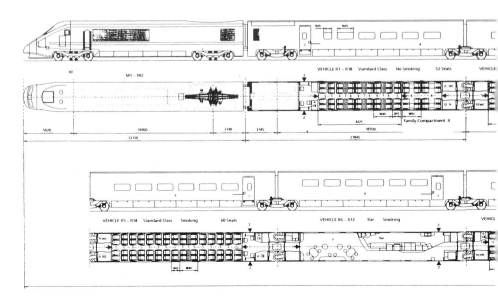

The TGV uses only one pantograph in ac mode which supplies current to both power cars through a cable along the roof of the train. Eurostar is much longer and each of its power cars has two retractable pantographs – a standard TGV 25,000 v ac and a specially-designed pantograph for collecting power from the Belgian lines.

Courtesy of Quadrant Picture Library.

Three different power supplies were involved. *Eurostar* therefore has to adapt to conditions and operates three different types of electrical power supply: 750 volts dc, with power collection by means of retractable shoegear from the third rail on the southern part of the UK rail system; 25,000 volts ac collected by an overhead catenary on the new high speed lines in France, Belgium, in the Channel Tunnel and on the conventional lines north of London; and 3,000 volts dc, requiring a separate overhead catenary on the conventional Belgian network. Despite these variations, the

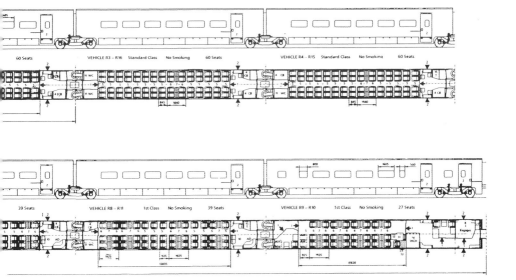

The Eurostar driving cab is one of the most sophisticated in the world. There is a computer console, 'cruise' speed-control, plus a number of different cab-signalling systems. The on-board computer system links the driver's braking and traction controls with the electronic systems which ensure that the current collection is supplied to the motors in both power cars at opposite ends of the train. The central position has little to do with left or right hand drive, but gives the driver a clearer all-round view. At speeds of 300 k.p.h., he cannot decipher trackside signals, but must rely on the computer and other signalling equipment.
Courtesy of EPS.

supply to feed power to the traction motors and to meet the train's lighting and heating demands is at consistent levels.

There are four different signalling systems involved, so drivers must know how each works. However, they do have help – *Eurostar* is equipped with an on-board signalling system and support systems. On the French high speed line and in the Tunnel there are no conventional line-side signals – the driver simply does not have time to read them. In consequence, an in-cab system, TVM 430, has been designed to pick up and decode data sent either by beacons or on the rails. The TVM 430 features a cab display which indicates the speed limits to be observed by the driver, in either miles or kilometres per hour, depending on the train's location. It also plots a speed-control curve and applies braking to the train if it exceeds the prescribed speed.

Eurostar's automatic coupling system means that trains can be divided in less than two minutes. In the event of a technical failure in one power car, it can be separated from the rest of the train, which will then be pushed by the other power car.

To reach and maintain a speed of 186 miles (300 kilometres) per hour, on the high speed lines, *Eurostar* is equipped with electrical induction motors mounted on each axle of the power cars as well as on the first two axles of each adjoining passenger-coach. A total of 12 motors are capable

When the train brakes from 186 miles an hour, it takes one minute five seconds to come to a complete halt, over a distance of just under three kilometres. In doing so, it absorbs as much energy as it takes to run a domestic electric fire non-stop for two weeks.

of developing a tractive power of 12,200 kw which is only used on the new high speed lines. On traditional lines, limits are set by the track layouts and the capacity of the electricity supply systems used. The traction motors and their reduction gearboxes, which provide the transmission to the axles, are mounted directly below the underframes of the power cars. This arrangement, which reduces the size of non-suspended masses, improves the dynamic behaviour of the train, and its impact on the track.

An exceptionally efficient braking system is required for trains which run at such speeds. *Eurostar* has a combination of three braking systems: on the non-powered axles, braking is provided by friction pads on four disks per axle; on the driving axles, by traction motors operating as current generators and, additionally, by the friction of brake shoes on the wheel treads. The current produced by the traction motors is directed towards the rheostats – devices which can regulate the flow of current – where it is dissipated. The advantage of this system is that the wheels absorb energy, which increases their service life. This type of rheostatic braking is also independent of any current supply and ensures maximum braking availability in all circumstances.

The passenger carriages are joined by twin axle bogies, the rear of one carriage riding on the front axle and the front of the adjoining carriage riding on the other. This means that there are no axles, bogies or wheels located beneath any of the passenger seating. It also means that it is possible to have less bogies, thus reducing energy consumption and saving weight. This articulated train moves as one, rather like a stiff rope and the bogie position means that the carriages do not sway, particularly where they join together. *Eurostar* also has an excellent pneumatic suspension system, ensuring a smooth ride.

Power car under construction at GEC Alsthom, Belfort, France. Each power car has 20 kilometres of wiring.
Courtesy of C. Whiting.

Bogies are positioned between trailers to give stability on the tracks. Each bogie has two axles and four wheels and is fitted with pneumatic suspension.
Courtesy of EPS.

TESTING

All the separate components which make up the *Eurostar* trains were continually tested during manufacture. Following delivery of the first completed *Eurostar* trainset in the early part of 1993 testing began on a test rig at Tournai, Belgium. It was then tested on the SNCB system between Ath and Silly on the Brussels-Tournai-Lille line. The priority was to ensure that *Eurostar* would not cause disruption to the existing signalling systems – fortunately it did not; although there were some relatively serious problems relating to the behaviour of the 3,000 v drive circuits, and manufacturers had to modify the computer software several times.

Eurostar *has 2 power cars and 18 coaches (14 for 'Beyond London' trains) and seating for 794 passengers.*

*Length:
394 meters
(1,292 feet)*

*Width:
2.8 metres (9.2 feet)*

*Weight when loaded:
800 tonnes*

*Tractive power:
around 12,200 kw – approximately 16,400 hp*

*Maximum speed:
186 miles
(300 kilometres)
per hour*

*Cost:
£24 million
(1988 prices)*

Eurostar *on test runs.*
Courtesy of EPS.

All high speed testing, which began in November 1993, had to take place in France, then the only network with a 300 kilometre-per-hour infrastructure. The first *Eurostar* to pass through the Channel Tunnel was a pre-series half trainset, known as PS1. Pulled by a diesel locomotive, as the electrical power supply had yet to be switched on, it made its journey to the English side on 20th June 1993. In February 1994, *Eurostar* was again tested in Belgium to ensure a smooth transition from the 3000 v dc of the country's conventional lines to the 25,000 v ac of high speed lines. The following month saw a changeover test from BR's 750 v dc network to the Tunnel's 25,000 v ac.

Traction performance, noise levels, fire detection and fire fighting devices, train-to-shore radio, the on-board TVM 430 signalling system, the

computers and even the coffee machines, were tested and tested again to meet the exacting standards and strict regulations of all three rail networks plus those of the Channel Tunnel, before the trains were finally allowed to operate.

Eurostar *trainsets under construction at GEC Alsthom, Belfort, France.* Courtesy of C. Whiting.

The nose of the train is designed to open for easy maintenance to the electrical wiring and mechanisms inside.
Courtesy of C. Whiting.

Eurostar *noses lined up for assembly at Belfort.*
Courtesy of C. Whiting.

T R A I N I N G

The decision of the three railways to run straight through between London and Paris and Brussels without a change of crew created its own problems and was made on business, operational and productivity grounds. There is little point in running at three miles a minute if you are then forced to stop for a five-minute crew changeover.

Eurostar is the most complex train in the world, operating within four different systems, in three different countries, at speeds of up to 300 kilometres per hour. Inevitably it requires the highest standard of driving and management, and for this, a new grade has been created: 'International Driver'. In Britain, European Passenger Service's first step was to advertise in *Rail News* (British Rail's staff paper), inviting BR drivers with at least five years' experience driving express trains to apply for a preliminary interview. About 400 responded, who then sat an aptitude test, which tested their powers of co-ordination, concentration and reaction speed. They all had to be not only technically competent but able to speak, or learn, French. By September 1992, 24 drivers had passed this test and a medical.

The drivers' and train managers' training programme soon gathered pace in all three countries. EPS's training programme eventually involved 94 drivers and 120 train managers, and the building of a new training establishment, next door to Waterloo Station in Holmes House. After a one-week induction course, drivers, train managers and other staff attended a French course at one of four London polytechnics (now universities). The teaching programme was specially designed towards the needs of the railway work and the different levels of staff. The EPS drivers also spent part of this time in Lille, living 'en famillle' with French families to improve their French and to learn about the culture, while their French and Belgian counterparts came to Britain. Drivers and crew take regular refresher courses. The on-board staff are able to speak French and English and, in some cases, Flemish and German.

After all this, and a week's psychological and psychometric testing, those that passed the assessments were offered contracts and further training.

The drivers' training programme lasted about 15 months, with 20 weeks of further language training spread through this time. Drivers were then taught about the different signalling and control systems and the rules of SNCF and SNCB as well as those of BR and Eurotunnel. This was done through a computer-aided learning programme. Much of the driving training was carried out on simulator, not unlike that used for training aircraft pilots. The drivers then moved on to the real thing, driving *Eurostars* here, in France and Belgium, during the thousands of miles of testing required for each train.

DRIVING THE TRAIN

Each *Eurostar* in operation has a crew of one driver and two train managers who are in charge throughout the return trip between Paris and London or London and Brussels. The cab resembles the cockpit of a jumbo jet and, like an aircraft pilot, the driver must complete a checklist, using an on-board tri-lingual computer system which provides information on the

Courtesy of EPS.

condition of the train, before starting out. During the journey, the driver can consult the computerised troubleshooting guide for information on how to correct any possible equipment failures and to check on any restrictions that apply. This information may also be sent by radio directly to the control centre at Lille; staff can then inform the maintenance centre of any problem, enabling repair engineers to prepare replacement parts or specialised equipment, even before the train arrives back at the depot.

Drivers use the language of the railway system the train is travelling through, but can also choose to speak in their mother-tongue on the train-to-shore radio link, which is compatible with the four different railway systems. They can also display instructions in their own language on the train's computer, making it easier to memorise information.

Using the same features developed for the TGV *Atlantique*, the on-board computer links the driver's braking system and traction controls with the electronic system which ensures that the correct current is supplied to the motors in both power cars at opposite ends of the train. The computer also controls the passenger information system in the train which displays the time of the train's departure, its destination and so on. In addition, the computer monitors information for alarm systems.

By placing the driver's position, or desk, in the centre of the cab, drivers benefit from all-round visibility.

IN THE TUNNEL

For the journey through the Tunnel, all trains operate under the Eurotunnel Control Centre. To comply with Channel Tunnel safety requirements, numerous changes were required to the design and construction materials

of the latest TGVs. One of the most important of these is the facility for the driver or train manager to divide the train in the Tunnel. This can happen in three places: each of the two power-cars can be uncoupled and, in addition, the train can be split between the two centre coaches. Automatic Scharfenberg couplers are used, released by hydraulic pump-levers from inside the coaches. The couplings, braking and services connections are compatible with Eurotunnel's diesel-electric locomotives, so that the *Eurostar* trains can be hauled out of the Tunnel should the power supply fail.

The trains are also equipped to communicate by radio with the Eurotunnel Control Centre. This equipment has to be tested and proved to be working before the train can enter the Tunnel. In addition, a train cannot enter the Tunnel if the power equipment on more than one bogie is out of action. Should there be a fire, a further safety features allows the driver to close the fresh-air intake and switch to the air-conditioning system, thus preventing smoke or fumes being sucked in. The materials used to build *Eurostar* are designed to withstand fire for up to 30 minutes – enough time for the train to be hauled out of the Tunnel. Should the driver be incapacitated, managers are specially trained to manoeuvre the train out.

Eurotunnel Control Centre
The controllers sit at three rows of desks with a 'mimic board' in front of them that shows the position of all trains and shuttles that are in the Tunnel at any one time. Signals are sent direct to the driver's cab and if a driver ignores them, the train will automatically slow down or stop. The control and communications systems are designed to continue operating in the event of a power cut. Rail traffic through the Tunnel is normally controlled from the Folkestone Control Centre. The Calais Control Centre acts as an emergency back-up and is fully staffed at all times. From time to time, controls are switched from Folkestone to Calais to check everything is working properly.
Courtesy of QA Photos Ltd, Hythe, Kent.

Inflatable door seals prevent sudden pressure variations in the Tunnel, which can occur particularly on entrance and exit, when the train's speed may reach 160 kilometres per hour.

CHAPTER THREE

ROUTES

BELGIUM

Initially, *Eurostar* uses the existing line 94. From 1997, it will travel on a new, high speed line between the French border and the outskirts of Brussels. This line passes to the south of Tournai, Leuze and Ath. It runs alongside the Ath-Enghien line and then alongside the A8 autoroute (Brussels-Lille) between Enghien and Tubize, where it joins another line at Lembeek. From the French border to Lembeek where the new line terminates, 17 kilometres from Brussels, the speed will be limited to 220 kilometres per hour up to the immediate outskirts of Brussels-Midi station.

FRANCE

Eurostar uses the Northern high speed line which goes from Gonesse, 16 kilometres outside Paris, as far as the entrance to the Tunnel, via Lille. The trains between London and Brussels use the Frethun-Lille section where the junctions between the French high speed line and the high speed line being built in Belgium are situated. Until this line comes into service, *Eurostar* will go from Lille to Brussels on conventional Belgian lines.

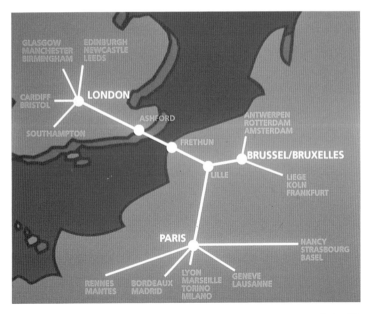

Courtesy of EPS.

GREAT BRITAIN

The existing lines between London and the Tunnel have been improved at a cost of £300 million, excluding the modifications to track circuits. This involved the re-construction of 94 bridges between Cheriton, Kent and London's Waterloo terminal; increasing power supplies; installing passing loops; and relocating, renewing or upgrading much of the present track. There has also been reinforcement of the electricity supply and new signalling between the Tunnel and Chislehurst, on the outskirts of London. Fully bi-directional signalling has been installed between the Tunnel and Ashford, the new international station in Kent, and the Tunnel, and simplified bi-directional signalling between Ashford and Sevenoaks. A new one kilometre-long curved viaduct between Waterloo International and the passenger routes to the Tunnel is the largest railway viaduct built in the UK this century.

Eurostar uses one main route from London to the Tunnel, travelling through Brixton in South London, to Bromley, Orpington, Sevenoaks, Tonbridge and Ashford in Kent. There are several alternatives which *Eurostar* can use in case of track repair or at busy times.

While *Eurostar* cannot travel at its top speeds from Waterloo to the Tunnel, a high speed line is envisaged between the Channel Tunnel and London, with another international terminal at the famous existing St Pancras station in north London. This line should be completed by 2002 and will allow improved journey times for trains going north of London.

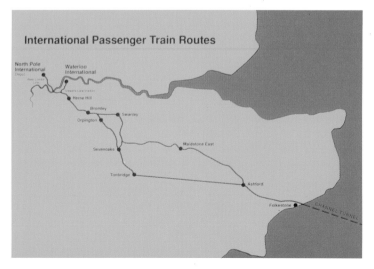

International Passenger Train Routes

Existing lines between Waterloo International and the Channel Tunnel, Folkestone. Courtesy of EPS.

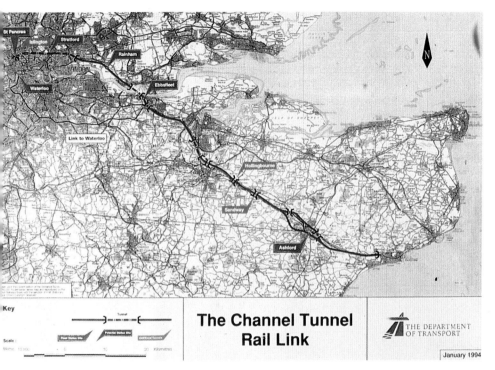

The Channel Tunnel Rail Link

The proposed high speed link.
Courtesy of EPS.

CHAPTER FOUR

THE TERMINALS

W A T E R L O O I N T E R N A T I O N A L LONDON

Waterloo International was completed on 17th May 1993, at a cost of £130 million. Built within the boundaries of the already busy Waterloo mainline station, it had taken 30 months. Part of the main station was in fact demolished to make way for the new terminal, a magnificent glass and steel building designed by Nicholas Grimshaw and Partners. It has four levels, with its five platforms at the top, covers an area of more than 7.5 acres, and comprises five 400 metre-long platforms, a new passenger terminal and lounges, 21 booking desks, restaurants, shops and currency exchange services.

Courtesy of EPS.

Courtesy of EPS.

The terminal has the capacity to handle more than 15 million passengers a year, with arriving and departing passengers separated at all times. Computer technology controls fire sprinklers, temperature and air conditions. The area is monitored by security video cameras.

The most striking feature of the terminal is the roof, with its glass and stainless steel cladding, supported on a network of tubular trusses. This dramatic tapering roof has 37 bow string arches varying in span from 32.7 metres to 48.5 metres, with an overall length of 400 metres. The natural light from the 10,000 square metres of glass is supplemented by station lights with automatic sensors. Designed to be a separate, but integral, part of the whole of Waterloo station, glass walls allow full view of the platforms from inside the mainline station.

Courtesy of EPS.

ASHFORD ENGLAND

A new international station at Ashford in Kent is under construction by John Laing PLC. It is expected that some two million passengers will use the new station, which will have 10 to 15 trains arriving and departing each day to and from Paris and Brussels. The scheme involves the redevelopment of the existing station site where the platforms have been extended to accommodate the *Eurostar* trains, and a new area is being built for South-Eastern domestic services. The site will also have car parking spaces for 2,000 cars.

Artist's impression.
Ashford International has been designed by Nick Derbyshire Design Associates Ltd. The terminal, with the capacity to handle 800 passengers, has two levels consisting of immigration and arrivals hall, ticket office and entrance concourse. The upper level has a departure lounge with shops, a café and security control. Arriving and departing passengers are kept separate by use of a subway for the former and a footbridge for the latter.
Courtesy of Ashford Borough Council.

GARE DU NORD PARIS

Gare Du Nord is considered one of Paris's historical monuments, but it too has undergone a complete facelift in honour of *Eurostar*. With its glass canopy cleaned, the station now fills with natural light. Even with all the new facilities and designer seating, it still has old-fashioned charm.

Half a million people use the Gare du Nord station daily. By the year 1998, the Eurostar terminal is expected to handle around 8.9 million passengers.

The four platforms reserved for Eurostar at Gare du Nord are enclosed and are only accessible from its terminal. Situated on the upper level of the station, the terminal comprises a waiting lounge, check-in section, customs controls and a boarding area. Each ticket is checked through an entry system to allow access to the terminal. Courtesy of SNCF.

B R U S S E L S - M I D I BELGIUM

Courtesy of SNCB – Presse et Relations Publiques

Belgium's Brussels-Midi has also been entirely renovated. More space, and better lighting and services have improved both the capacity and amenities for passengers. 28 new escalators have been installed and the noise level in the station is reduced by double acoustics cover over the tracks.

CHAPTER FIVE

BEYOND THE THREE CAPITALS

Initially, *Eurostar* will run beyond London, with seven 14-coach trains. These trains have to be shorter in length – 320 metres (578 seats and 36 tip-up seats) – in order to use the shorter platforms of Britain's other major city stations. As the service is phased in over the next few years, the international network to and from Paris and Brussels will extend to Manchester, Birmingham and Edinburgh, and include other major stations en route.

Beyond London daytime trains are built to much the same technical specifications as the main *Eurostar* trains; a few amendments have been incorporated in order to prevent signalling interference and to work with Railtrack's electrification system.

Typical journey times will be:

Edinburgh to Paris:	8 hours
Edinburgh to Brussels:	8.15 hours
Manchester to Paris:	5.45 hours
Manchester to Brussels:	6.30 hours
Birmingham International to Paris:	4.30 hours
Birmingham International to Brussels:	4.45 hours

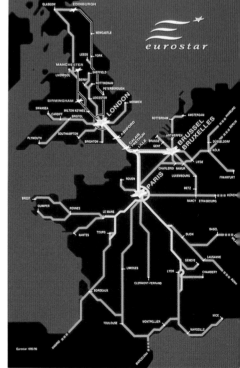

Journey times to Brussels will be shortened by half an hour when Belgium's high speed line opens in 1997.

As more high speed lines open up across Europe, *Eurostar* will be able to extend its service and offer journeys to other destinations in Europe – from Edinburgh to the south of France, Germany, Italy and Spain. In order to create a cohesive network, the railways of each member of the European Union, plus Austria and Switzerland, have already agreed to take steps technically and commercially to harmonise their systems and infrastructure.

Courtesy of EPS.

CHAPTER SIX

NIGHT SERVICES

The Channel Tunnel connects Britain's 16,000 kilometres of track with the 185,000 kilometres of standard gauge track in continental Europe.

Work is already underway to provide not only other city centre to city centre day trains, but also a night service – a new generation of international hotel trains, revolutionising long distance overnight travel in Europe. Go to bed in Plymouth or Swansea and wake up in Paris.

Two groups of overnight services will be offered. Initially, there will be regional night trains from Swansea, Plymouth and Glasgow to Paris. London-based night trains will also run from Waterloo to Amsterdam, and to Cologne, Dortmund and Frankfurt.

EPS and its partners awarded GEC Alsthom/Metro Cammell Ltd the £120 million contract in June 1992 to build these trains. There are three different types of coach, although each is 23 metres long and capable of operating at 200 kilometres per hour where track conditions permit. Each train will carry about 400 passengers, most travelling in comfortable reclining seats. There are also cabins, all of which include a hand basin and toilet and many have showers. The service car contains a catering area and bar with a plush lounge where light snacks and drinks will be served. There will also be accommodation on board for train crew and Customs officers and a storage room for bicycles and skis. The service is due to start towards the end of 1995.

As the service expands, it will soon be possible to travel between most major cities in Britain and mainland Europe – without changing trains.
Courtesy of EPS.

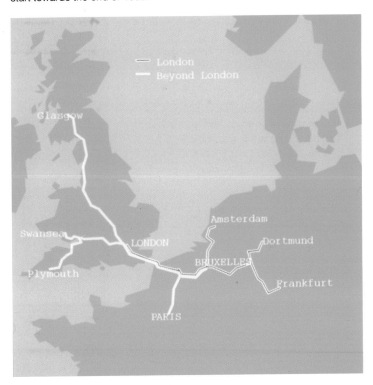

CHAPTER SEVEN

BEHIND THE SCENES

NORTH POLE INTERNATIONAL DEPOT

The trains need daily cleaning and regular servicing. This is not practical within the terminals, so special depots have been developed in all three countries: at Le Landy, Paris, Brussels Forest; and at North Pole Depot, West London. Rail access from Waterloo is over the West London line. The strangely-named North Pole depot cost £80 million and is three kilometres long and about 70 metres wide. It has its own signalling system to control the complex track layout.

It is here that each *Eurostar* train remaining in Britain overnight will

North Pole Depot covers six railway tracks and is as wide as the Cunard Liner, Queen Elizabeth II.
Courtesy of EPS.

Over 200 personnel man the sheds on a shift basis. All of them have to pass an extensive safety training programme.
Courtesy of EPS.

come for servicing. The train passes through a washing plant and moves on to have its toilets discharged; it then spends about two hours in the servicing shed where the power supplies are examined while the train is cleaned inside from nose to tail. Finally, it moves to a siding in readiness for the next day's work. A shed for major repairs is located on the east side of the depot. On average, 12 or 13 *Eurostar* trains will be processed here each night, although the depot can cater for up to 18 trains at a time.

The carriage washer cleans the carriages and the front of the trains. The lavatory retention tanks also require discharging – a process which takes approximately 30 minutes.
Courtesy of EPS.

The whole depot is very tight on security, with close circuit television of the entire site, and extensive radio and telephone communications throughout. Trespassers risk being exposed to electrified track and overhead electrical systems.
Courtesy of EPS.

CHAPTER EIGHT

THE TUNNEL

An international high speed train service joining Britain to the European mainland would not have been possible without the building of the Channel Tunnel. With the Straits of Dover a mere 21 miles across at its narrowest, the concept of a link between Britain and France is not new; however, it is one that has caused controversy for almost 200 years. Britain's pride in being an island, its fear of invasion and a history of war between the two countries created the feeling that it was not in either country's interest to be joined together.

Cartoon, published around the 1800s, showing an invasion of England by a fleet of troop-carrying balloons and an army of infantry and artillery moving through a tunnel under the Channel.

By 1802, the Peace of Amiens treaty seemed to have ended the years of conflict between France and England and Bonaparte took great interest in plans for a Channel tunnel, submitted by French engineer Albert Mathieu-Favier. Using traditional mining techniques, Mathieu envisaged that passengers would travel in horse-drawn coaches in an undersea tunnel ventilated by huge iron chimneys. Although not based on any sound geological studies, these plans are generally acknowledged as the first serious proposal for a Channel tunnel. They were short-lived as, within a year, war had again broken out between the two countries.

Albert Mathieu's scheme for a Channel tunnel, 1802.

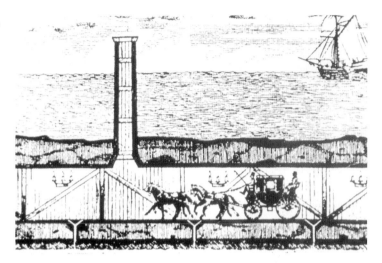

Some years later, another Frenchman, Joseph-Aimé Thomé de Gamond, became fascinated with the idea of a fixed link and took up Mathieu's almost forgotten plans. In 1834, at the age of 27, he proposed the laying of iron tubes, lined with brick, in sections across the Straits of Dover, but cost soon proved prohibitive. He then proposed an iron Channel bridge, followed by a plan for a floating bridge and another for a bridge resting on granite piles. He also suggested 'narrowing' the Channel by two jetties, each eight kilometres long, using huge steam-powered boats to ferry passengers and freight between the two jetties. Such plans were quickly abandoned, due to cost and danger to shipping. Inspired by Sir Marc Isambard Brunel, who had built the tunnel under the River Thames, de Gamond then put forward a proposal for a tunnel which would run via an artificial island on the Varne Bank in mid-Channel.

Thomé de Gamond's design for a bored tunnel with an artificial maritime station on the Varne Bank mid-Channel. He estimated its cost as 170 million gold francs (then equivalent to about £8.5 million).

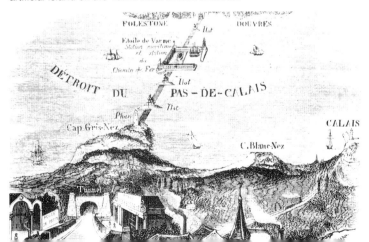

This plan foundered like the others, but it did
succeed in provoking the interest of British
engineer, William Low, who had experience in
mining. Low was able to identify de Gamond's
problems of ventilation, and concluded that the
Tunnel was indeed feasible. He joined forces with
two other British engineers, James Brunlees and
John Hawkshaw, and, in 1872, they registered
their company as The Channel Tunnel Company
Limited. By 1882, a tunnel of 1.85 kilometres (1.15
miles) had been bored from Shakespeare Cliff but
fear of invasion again put a stop to the work. The
French, who had their own Tunnel Company, gave
up hope of the British continuing with the project
and ordered their own construction force at
Sangatte, near Calais, to stop.

The 1880s scheme was resurrected in the
1920s but technical hitches and a general lack of
support meant that it progressed no further than
trial borings. Work was not restarted in earnest
until 1974 and then only after every conceivable
type of other link had been studied and dismissed.

With war in the Middle East creating an oil
crisis and a climate of economic uncertainty, the
British Government abandoned the project a third
time. But it was not to be forgotten. In 1981,
François Mitterrand and Margaret Thatcher agreed
that a fixed cross-channel link would be beneficial
to both countries and yet more studies were
commissioned. A consortium of British banks and
construction companies began negotiating with
their French counterparts, France-Manche. Yet
another Anglo-French Treaty was signed in 1986,
and at last work began at Sangatte. The following
year, the newly-merged international company,
Trans Manche Link (TML) sank its first shaft at
Shakespeare Cliff.

Engineers had always favoured the
Shakespeare Cliff-to-Sangatte route, partly
because the Channel is at its narrowest point here,

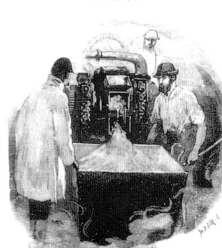

In 1882, the Illustrated London News *published four pages of
pictures and a report on the first press and VIP visits to the tunnel
workings.*

and partly because there is a layer of chalk marl that runs almost all the way across. Marl, a mixture of chalk and clay, is soft and easy to tunnel through; unlike chalk, it is more or less waterproof, and strong enough not to collapse when holes are bored through it. When the 1880s tunnel at Shakespeare Cliff was reopened almost a century later, it was still dry and in good condition, despite never having been lined.

The two ends of the service tunnel eventually met mid-Channel at 7.30 pm on 30th October 1990, if only by a probe. The official breakthrough ceremony took place on the 1st December when a thin chalk diaphragm was drilled through by Englishman Graham Fagg and he disappeared through a hole to be greeted by French miner, Philippe Cozette. Great Britain had ceased to be an island.

The Channel Tunnel was officially declared open by Her Majesty Queen Elizabeth II and President Mitterrand on 6th May 1994. After years of delay, and at a cost of almost £9 billion, it was an engineering, and political miracle.

The historic moment of breakthrough.
Courtesy of QA Photos Ltd, Hythe, Kent.

The two ends of the service tunnel were joined by a probe on October 30th, but it was the official opening ceremony, to which Queen Elizabeth II travelled on Eurostar, that created world-wide interest. It was just three years since work had begun on the British undersea service tunnel.
Courtesy of EPS.

With the service trains connected up behind them, tunnel boring machines were longer than two football pitches.
Courtesy of QA Photos Ltd, Hythe, Kent.

CONSTRUCTION

- During every eight-hour shift, up to 1,000 people were transported to their underground workplace by the construction railway.

- For safety reasons, engineers had to have a working knowledge of technical terms in both French and English.

- Huge tunnel boring machines (TBMs) were purpose-built, the largest 8.78 metres (28.17 feet) in diameter, weighing 1, 575 tonnes.

- The teeth of the TBM cutting heads were made of tungsten carbide, able to cut through the chalk marl at up to one kilometre (0.62 miles) per month.

- TBMs were kept on course using laser beams. The on-board cabin computers reacted to the laser beams and plotted the exact position.

- Conveyor belts carried the 2,400 tonnes of spoil (fragments of rocks and marl), collected every hour from the cutting head, to the supply train which took it out of the tunnel. On the British side, a sea wall was extended at the foot of the site and the spoil was dumped into the resulting artificial lagoon. On the French side, spoil was crushed and mixed with water to form slurry. A huge dam was built on top of a hill, and the slurry was pumped into the artificial lake created by the dam. Once the lake had dried out, it was landscaped and grassed over.

- The tunnel is lined with rings made of concrete segments, which are sealed together with cement grout. Cast iron linings were installed at weaker points and at cross-passage junctions.

- After tunnelling was complete, the construction railway tracks were removed and a concrete floor laid for the standard 4-foot 8.5-inch railway track. 334,000 special concrete fixing blocks with shock absorbers were used to secure the track.

Aerial shot of the Folkestone Terminal.
Courtesy of QA Photos Ltd, Hythe, Kent.

The Tunnel includes two huge cross-over tunnels (the one shown here is on the British side and has not had its doors put in place), where trains can change from one track to the other. If one tunnel had to be closed for maintenance or repair, trains would be delayed. The cross-over caverns mean that only a section of the tunnel need be out of service at any one time. To change from one tunnel to another, trains have to slow down to less than 60 kilometres (38 miles) per hour. *Courtesy of EPS.*

TECHNICAL SPECIFICATIONS

- The Channel Tunnel is in fact three parallel tunnels. Two are rail tunnels, for traffic in each direction. A third tunnel is for service use, with a diameter of 16 feet, through which diesel-powered wheeled service vehicles run.

- The three tunnels are connected by cross passages every 375 metres (1,230 feet).

- At around 46 metres below sea level, there are two huge cross-over caverns, where trains can change, if need be, from one line to another.

- Fresh air is pumped at 144 cubic metres (5,085 cubic feet) a second down the service tunnel – enough for 20,000 people to breathe.

- Two cooling pipes run through each train tunnel.

- There are three pumps, two in Britain, one in France, to pump out any water that might seep in. They have a drainage capacity of 153 litres (34 gallons) per second.

SAFETY MEASURES

- *Control centres have direct contact with the emergency services.*

- *Sophisticated communications systems on rolling stock enable the control centres to communicate with the train, and the driver or train manager to communicate with passengers.*

- *Staff are trained in emergency procedures and there are regular practices of simulated incidents.*

- *If a train is halted in the Tunnel for any reason, other trains can be brought out without delay and staff ensure that all passengers, including those on the stranded train, can reach open air within 90 minutes maximum. Cross passages provide access for emergency services and passenger evacuation.*

- *All passenger trains are required to have two locomotives – one at each end – so that in the event of one failing, the other can push or pull the train out of the Tunnel. In addition, there are diesel locomotives on standby to deal with the remote possibility of a failure of both national grid supplies.*

- *Electrical power for the tunnel system, for drainage pumps, lighting and other services is duplicated on separate circuits from both sides of the Channel. Eurotunnel also has its own standby auxiliary power supply for emergency situations.*

- *The two separate running tunnels virtually eliminate any possibility of a head-on collision.*

- *Gas and petroleum tankers, cargoes of liquid petroleum, nuclear waste, dangerous chemicals and highly volatile or inflammable products are forbidden passage through the Tunnel.*

- *Every day, 2.5 million readings are taken from the Tunnel's 500 sensors which analyse and check environmental conditions.*

- *Automatic fire detectors and suppression systems are located in underground technical rooms along the length of the tunnel.*

- *There are fire hydrants at cross passages and in the running tunnels, an automatic foam system for dealing with fires beneath vehicles, and an automatic or manual halon gas system if a fire survives other measures.*

- *All rolling stock, including* Le Shuttle *and* Eurostar, *has been designed using fire-resistant materials which minimise any fire risk or emission of toxic fumes and smoke. Wherever practicable, materials and equipment, including cables, are similarly designed.*

- *A highly sophisticated ventilation system ensures that there is enough fresh air in the Tunnel. In the event of emergency, there is a separate supplementary ventilation system which will be used in conjunction with the normal one.*

- *A cooling system maintains the air temperature.*

- *Pumping systems can deal with any water seepage, damaged water mains, rain on the rolling stock, and if necessary, for fire fighting.*

- *All tunnels and connecting passages have sufficient lighting for operational, maintenance and emergency purposes. The fixed lighting installations can be switched on from the control centres or from points within the tunnels. The tunnels are never in complete darkness.*

- *In the event of a train driver failing to react to automatic signalling indications, the system will override the driver and slow or stop the train.*

- *A high level of security is maintained in the Tunnel and in all depot and station areas.*

THE SERVICE

- *Journey time is 35 minutes from terminal to terminal*

- *At peak times, trains travel every three minutes at up to 160 kilometres (100 miles) per hour.*
- *There can be seven or eight trains in the tunnel at any one time.*

- *Unaffected by weather, the Tunnel operates 24 hours a day, 52 weeks a year.*

Eurotunnel's electric locomotive Le Shuttle *which carries vehicles and freight through the Tunnel at a speed of 160 kilometres per hour.*

- Le Shuttle's *eight freight, and nine passenger-vehicle trains operate on a loop line, using the same tracks as* Eurostar.

- *The Channel Tunnel is the longest undersea tunnel. The Seikan Tunnel in Japan is longer overall, but only 23.3 kilometres (14.3 miles) is under the sea.*

- *Overall length: 50.45 kilometres (31.35 miles)*

- *Length under the sea: 38 kilometres (24 miles)*

- *Distance beneath the sea bed: between 45 and 75 metres (148 feet and 246 feet)*

Eurostar *emerging from the British (above) and French (below) ends of the Tunnel.* Courtesy of EPS.

Aerial view of Waterloo International, London, where passengers begin their journey. Courtesy of EPS.

CHAPTER NINE

EUROSTAR - THE EXPERIENCE

At 8 am, on a wet winter's morning, a day when high winds caused the cancellation of all Channel ferry crossings, I checked into Waterloo International to board the awaiting 8.23 London to Paris. After putting my ticket through the automatic barrier and my luggage through security, I entered the departure lounge. I changed some money at the Bureau de Change, bought a delicious coffee and sat down to await the announcement, in both English and French, that we could board the train.

I put my coat in the overhead luggage rack, sank into my very comfortable seat in first class, and picked up a copy of *Eurostar's* first special edition of its magazine. When everyone was settled, the automatic doors closed. It was only when I looked up from the magazine that I realised we were moving – the train is uncannily smooth and quiet. As we passed through the suburbs of London, breakfast was served, with proper cutlery – tea or coffee, fresh orange juice, fruit, croissant or *pain au chocolate,* and, if you had room, a full cooked English breakfast. Customs officers, who have their own office on board, walked the length of the train checking passports.

It was not long before the train manager announced that we were about to enter the Tunnel and that we should adjust our watches to French time – one hour ahead. As we sped through the darkness, I went to check out the seats for business meetings, with their cleverly-designed central folding tables and side lights. Just 20 minutes later, we emerged into the weak French sunlight. Accepting the offered glass of champagne, I listened to the announcement that we had reached our maximum speed of 300 kilometres per hour. The wine in my glass hardly rippled.

Around me, businessmen and women worked or read in silence – apart from the occasional tapping of laptops or the ringing of mobile phones. Outside, in the flat landscape, French farmers stopped to gaze and wave.

I walked into the futuristic-looking buffet where passengers were buying refreshments, paying in either Francs or sterling. Rightly proud of their train, the helpful, knowledgeable staff answered the many questions on it, in the language in which they were asked.

In standard class I bumped into a friend, who has businesses in London and Paris. I asked him what he thought of *Eurostar.* 'It's excellent,' he told me. 'And so convenient. I've used it regularly since the service started and it has always been on time. I have three uninterrupted hours in which to read or work, unlike travelling by air. I have enough time in Paris for lunch and for a meeting and can be back home in time for dinner. I won't travel any other way to Paris now.'

The train manager announced that we were almost at Gare du Nord station in the heart of Paris. We glided to a halt. The journey had taken just three hours. It had seemed like ten minutes.

Courtesy of Telegraph Colour Library.

CHAPTER TEN
CAPTURING THE SPIRIT

Throughout the history of modern transport, it is the train which has had the most profound effect on society. Apart from providing crucial links between families and friends, industries and commerce, the railways enable us to discover the heart and soul of a country at a speed and ease no other form of transport can achieve. The railways have inspired novelists, song writers, poets and film makers. Now *Eurostar*, perhaps the greatest and most significant train yet, has become the subject of a television film through the imagination of film director Peter Akehurst.

Courtesy of Anna Maria Valentini.

The film idea was based on a very ambitious plan to place a camera on the nose of a *Eurostar* train running between Waterloo Station in London and Gare du Nord Station in Paris, which would show the driver's view all the way. It was not an easy task. Several dummy runs had to be made to test the air pressure and strength of the camera box: it had to be able to withstand the impact of a large bird such as a pigeon or pheasant hitting it at 300 kilometres per hour. The holding bracket for the camera box was built by EPS engineers using high grade tensile stainless steel; while the camera box itself was designed and built by one of Peter Akehurst's engineers, and reflected the same body component for the outer skin with a ¾-inch optical glass to protect the camera lens. A very sophisticated wash/wipe system was needed to keep the glass clean.

The camera recording system chosen for this project was digital betacam; this, coupled with the very best broadcast camera available, allowed the pictures to be speeded up 18 times without any loss of picture quality.

The twin digital recorders were too large to set up in the driver's cabin and had to be placed in the first carriage of the train some 150 feet from the camera. This created another safety problem: how to get the two cables from the camera to the recorders. The problem was eventually solved by placing the small optical block from the back of the camera in the motor unit and then wiring down the outside of the train into the first carriage door.

All the setting up was done at the North Pole depot in west London. The complete camera/recording system took eight hours to set up and four hours to remove, involving a great many late nights. Filming for the high speed sequence took place in the latter part of 1994, which unfortunately turned out to be exeptionally wet and windy. Water leaks in the camera box and other unforeseen problems meant that it took eight attempts in all. However, with a great deal of patience and a dedicated crew this historic piece of filming was finally completed. The result is quite haunting and magical, truly capturing the spirit of this remarkable train.

Courtesy of Anna Maria Valentini.

THE CREW

PETER AKEHURST	Producer/Director, Wizard Productions
ANNA MARIA VALENTINI	Production Manager
ALAN STEVENS	Cameraman
JOHN HILLS-HARRUP	Soundman
TEX CHILDS	Chief Grip
RON OSMAN	Chief Electronic Engineer
GERRY ARNOLD	EPS Engineer
MEL FIDLIN	EPS Engineer

SOURCES

The Channel Tunnel: A 21st Century Transport System, published by The Channel Tunnel Group Ltd

The Department of Transport

European Passenger Service staff and publications. Telesales: 01233 617575

Eurotunnel

Garratt, Colin, *Britain's Railways: the Only Transport for the Future*, published by Sunburst Books

GEC Alsthom

Hedges, Martin (ed.), *150 years of British Railways*, published by The Hamlyn Publishing Group Ltd

Hunt, Donald, *The Tunnel: The Story of the Channel Tunnel 1802-1994*, published by Images Publishing (Malvern) Ltd

Modern Railways magazine

The Official Channel Tunnel Factfile, published by Boxtree

Perren, Brian, *TGV Handbook*, published by Capital Transport

Rail magazine

Railtrack